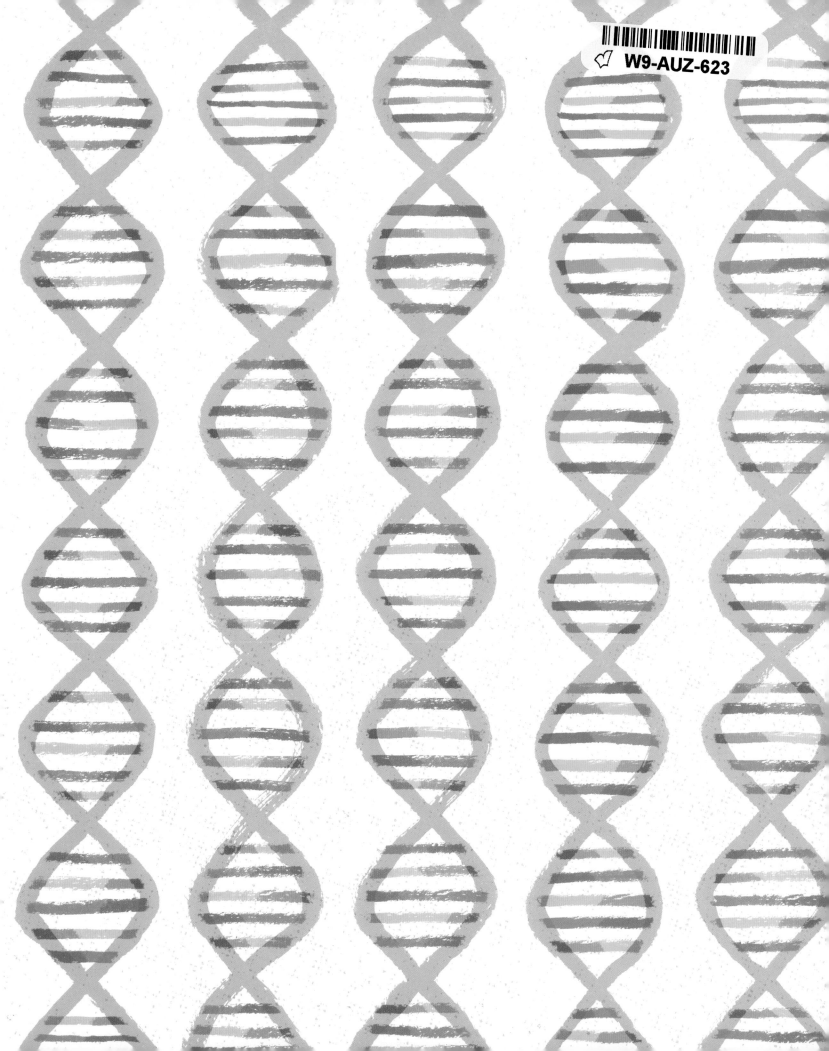

For Adam, Colin, and
Christopher — my favorite
bunch of DNA molecules. xo
— P.T.

For Madeline
— G.P.

Acknowledgments:
The author would like to thank
Simone Bender, Libby Lennie,
Christine Burkitt, Suzanne Bickford,
Kate Marshall Flaherty, Stacey Kondla,
Sam Hiyate, Barbara Berson,
Rotem Moscovich, and Chris Wallace.

THIS IS A BORZOI BOOK PUBLISHED BY ALFRED A. KNOPF

Text copyright © 2023 by Pauline Thompson • Jacket art and interior illustrations copyright © 2023 by Greg Pizzoli • All rights reserved. Published in the United States by Alfred A. Knopf, an imprint of Random House Children's Books, a division of Penguin Random House LLC, New York. • Knopf, Borzoi Books, and the colophon are registered trademarks of Penguin Random House LLC. • Visit us on the Web! rhcbooks.com • Educators and librarians, for a variety of teaching tools, visit us at RHTeachersLibrarians.com

Library of Congress Cataloging-in-Publication Data is available upon request.
ISBN 978-0-593-42704-0 (trade)—ISBN 978-0-593-42705-7 (lib. bdg.)—ISBN 978-0-593-42706-4 (ebook)

The text of this book is set in 14-point KG HAPPY Solid. • The illustrations were created using a black Pentel pocket brush pen on Fabriano mixed media paper. The individual drawings were then scanned and colored in Photoshop • Book design by Rachael Cole

MANUFACTURED IN CHINA • April 2023 • 10 9 8 7 6 5 4 3 2 1 • First Edition

Hooray for DNA!

How a Bear and a Bug Are a Lot Like Us

By **Pauline Thompson**

Illustrated by **Greg Pizzoli**

Alfred A. Knopf
New York

DNA is the ABC
of what makes you, you
and what makes me, me.

It's the set of instructions
for all life constructions,
from a bird to a bee and a tree.

What has two eyes, two ears,
a mouth, and a nose?

Can you think of things
that have all of those?

And teeth, and fingers,
and wiggly toes?

We're all connected.
That's just how it goes!

DNA dwells in the heart of all cells.

Building tissues and organs is
where it excels.

Without tissues and organs,
you're just a big blob.

And to make a whole person is DNA's job.

IT'S OUR SHARED DNA THAT . . .

Makes you part bear
and a hoppity hare.

It makes you a mammal,
part llama and camel.

It makes you part bat
and a calico cat,

a cougar, a crane,
and a common gray rat.

BAT

COUGAR

CRANE

And the whole wacky lot of us?

Part hippopotamus!

You,

me,

a bug,

and even a virus

have shared DNA
hidden inside us!

DNA builds life with
four chemical bricks.

It's all in the order that
makes for the mix.

GO
GULLS!

DINO
DNA!

With four colored LEGO,
you can build any shape.

With DNA bricks,
you can build a great ape.

It's really quite funky—

you're almost a monkey!

Our shared DNA bricks make us related.

The sequence is key for what is created.

The same DNA is needed to make
the spine inside you
and the spine in a snake.

IT'S OUR SHARED DNA THAT . . .

Makes you part beagle
and a soaring bald eagle.

It makes you part moose
and a kooky gray goose.

A ferret, a parrot,
a crunchy cashew—

it's nutty that they
share your DNA, too.

And just for a laugh,

you're part giraffe!

We share many features
with all living creatures.

But there's one that's identical,
less point one percentical.

IT'S . . .

People, all humans,
it's us—you and me!

Our shared DNA
makes us all family.

READING
ROCKETS!

Put aside language,
and culture, and race.

It's a DNA speck that
gives you your face.

A DNA speck gives you
brown eyes or blue.

A DNA speck gives your
skin color, too.

READING
ROCKETS

Less point one percent,
we're almost exact.

Almost DNA twins.
That's a DNA fact.

DNA is the code to build all living things,
from people to trees,
to birds with big wings.

DNA makes me, me.
DNA makes you, you.

And a bear and a bug—
and all of us, too.

GO
GULLS!

Hip hip hooray for our shared DNA!

WHAT MAKES DNA SO SPECIAL?

You are alive, right here, right now, reading this book, somewhere on planet Earth. You are a living miracle! Most scientists agree that for something to be alive, it has to have DNA—deoxyribonucleic acid (pronounced dee-ox-ee-RYE-bo-new-CLAY-ick acid). DNA is a clever little molecule found in the heart of all living cells, in all living things. Can you think of some things that are alive and some things that are not? How is a wood table different from a tree? Or a rock from a rhinoceros?

We live in a universe that is made up of atoms—tiny particles that form all the known elements of living and non-living things. You are a package of uniquely bundled atoms. (But you would need a very special microscope to see them.) A rock is a unique bundle of atoms, too. However, it is not alive. It does not have cells with DNA. And you do!

DNA is a chemical molecule made up of atoms. When atoms bond together, they form chemical compounds. For example, when two hydrogen atoms and an oxygen atom combine, they make water! DNA is a molecule, or chemical compound, made up of carbon, hydrogen, nitrogen, oxygen, and phosphorus.

Maybe you've heard you're mostly made of water? That's because of all the oxygen and hydrogen bonded together in your body. Maybe you've also heard the term carbon life-form? Well, that's you! You're a carbon life-form. As are plants and penguins. When you add some carbon to water, you have the very best ingredients for making life. But without DNA issuing the instructions, you're still not alive.

WHY DOES DNA MAKE YOU ALIVE?

DNA is the big boss, the grand master of *every cell* in your body. It tells cells what to do, how to do it, and when to stop doing what it's doing. DNA tells your body how to eat and use food energy, how to make more people, how to grow bigger, how to react to the world around you, how to keep your inside temperature steady, and how to put all the bits and pieces of you together to make you the person you are. If you want to dig deeper, the bigger names for all these DNA duties are metabolism, reproduction, growth, reactivity, homeostasis, and organization. It is because of all these DNA duties that you are alive—and a rock is not!

WHAT DOES DNA LOOK LIKE?

DNA lengths vary in every living thing. In humans, it looks like a twisted, six-foot-long ladder. That long ladder is then coiled into a tight little spring that you can't even see on the head of a pin! That's how DNA squeezes into the nucleus of every cell.

Each strand of DNA contains 3 billion instructions for building a person. Only about 3 million of those instructions make people different from each other. Think of a LEGO tower that is one hundred pieces tall. What makes you different from someone else is not even one piece of LEGO in that tower. It's just a small sliver of that one LEGO brick! We are so much more alike than we are different from each other.

DNA is at work, *all the time*, helping the miracle that is you to live, learn, and play *every day*. Hooray for DNA!

DNA SCAVENGER HUNT

We share a lot of DNA with all life on the planet. Search the web to find out how much DNA humans share with these living things. And think about what you have in common with them.

A grape? 24% shared DNA. Humans and grapes have skin. (To get you started.)

A chimpanzee?	A chicken?	A zebra fish?
A mouse?	A dog?	A horse?
A fruit fly?	A cow?	Yeast?
A banana?	A slug?	A platypus?
A tree?	A honeybee?	A roundworm?
A cat?	Rice?	A person?

EXPLORE SOME MORE!

Books

Grow: Secrets of Our DNA by Nicola Davies and Emily Sutton
A beautifully illustrated picture book that focuses on how living things grow and change differently, depending on their DNA.

The Secret Code Inside You: All About Your DNA by Rajani LaRocca and Steven Salerno
A picture book that simply explains heredity and why DNA makes us different from other creatures.

Videos

"DNA/Science/BrainPOP"

youtube.com/watch?v=kYlzJmJbN6A

Cartoon characters Tim and Moby give a great overview of DNA.

"A Neuroscientist Tries to Teach Kids About DNA Using Legos"

youtube.com/watch?v=BKolxUpppvE

An engaging live-action conversation for all ages. Also has activities.

"What Makes YOU YOU? What Makes ME ME?"

amnh.org/explore/ology/genetics/what-makes-you-you2

A playful overview from the American Museum of Natural History.

Websites

The American Museum of Natural History—"The Gene Scene"

amnh.org/explore/ology/genetics

This site has helpful general information, videos, games, stories, and activities. Lots to explore.

Britannica Kids article on DNA

kids.britannica.com/kids/article/DNA/390730

A factual site for older kids.

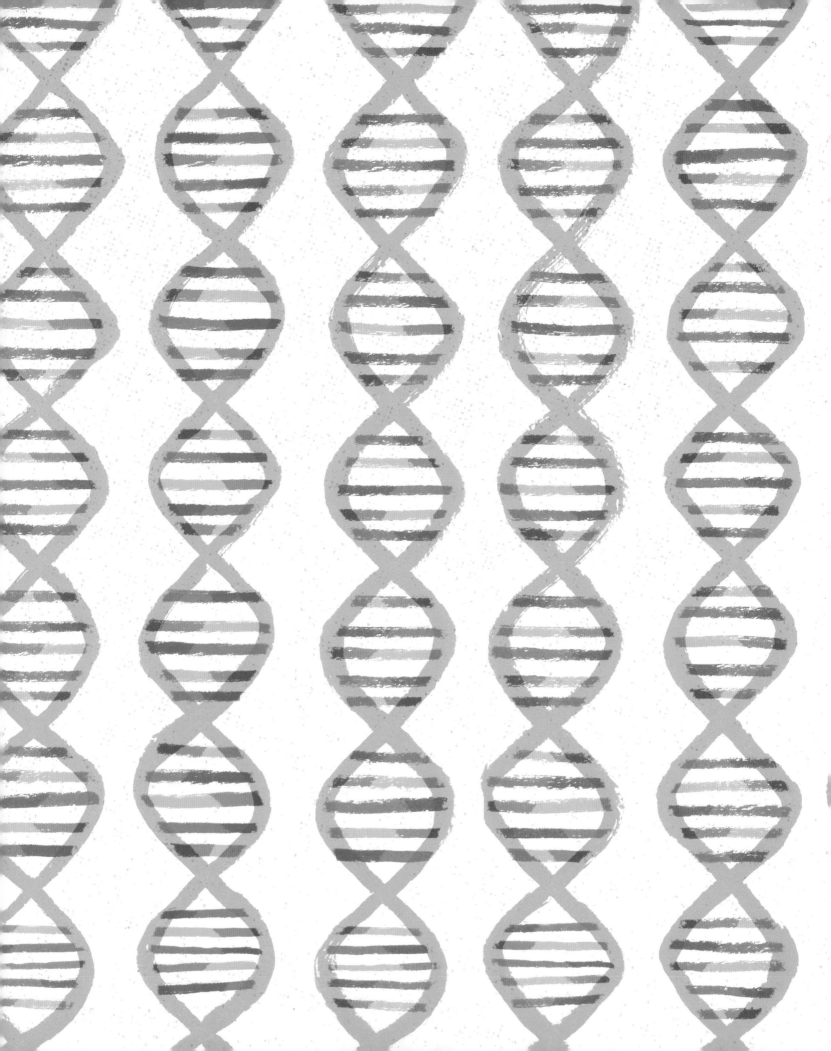